RULE AND REIGN YOUR INTERNAL WORLD:

DEFEATING ANXIETY

Youth/Adult Emotional Maturity Series

Angie G Meadows MS, RN

Sarah J Meadows BS

Angie G Meadows MS, RN, Sarah J Meadows BS

ABSTRACT

Ruling and Reigning our internal world through developmental emotional maturity skills halts toxic emotions that cause anxiety. This emotional ability mimics physical developmental skills. As a child grows physically, they learn to roll over, sit up, crawl, walk and then run. The development of emotions can be stunted or undeveloped and need to be matured and nurtured through intentional training and disciplining our intellect and thinking to support, nurture and master our emotions. Conquering anxiety, finding a safe self internally, learning to break a helpless/victim trap with disciplined thinking, uncovering hidden emotions under the cloak of anxiety, overcoming double-mindedness and internally finding rest and peace are just a few developmental emotional skills to rule and reign over our internal world. **(This is the same information as the Rock of Recovery Series for Enablers and those with Substance Use Disorder. It is reorganized for anyone needing Developmental Emotional Maturity Skills.)** This series is an individual devotional, home-school, or Christian School curriculum, Family Devotions, or Small Group anxiety study.

RULE AND REIGN YOUR INTERNAL WORLD: DEFEATING ANXIETY

A Thousand Tears, LLC
PO Box 561
Lewisburg, PA 17837
enablersjourney@gmail.com
www.angiegmeadows.com
www.enablersjourney.com

Rock of Recovery Podcast https://feed.podbean.com/rockofrecovery/feed.xml
Angie G Meadows YouTube https://youtu.be/7dkcrvCpS0s

The Podcast/YouTube is for the recovery version of the material. Stay tuned for audio/visual lessons of this material.

© 2020 Angie G. Meadows
All rights reserved. Except Permission is granted for non-commercial use, reproduction, and distribution for the purposes of Christian evangelism and discipleship. All other rights reserved.
Cover © Perry Meadows, 2020

This book is intended as general information only and should not be used to diagnose or treat any health condition. Considering the complex, individual, and specific nature of health problems, this book is not intended to replace professional medical advice. The ideas, procedures, and suggestions in this book are intended to supplement, not replace, the advice of a trained medical professional. Consult your physician before adopting any of the suggestions in this book, as well as about any condition that may require diagnosis or medical attention. The author and publisher disclaim any liability arising directly or indirectly from the use of this book.

This publication is designed to provide accurate and authoritative information regarding the subject matter covered. It is sold with the understanding that the publisher is not engaged in rendering legal, accounting, or other professional advice. If legal advice or other expert assistance is required, the services of a competent professional person should be sought.

From a *Declaration of Principles* jointly adopted by a Committee of the American Bar Association and a Committee of Publishers and Associations.

Contents

Rule and reign your internal WorlD: 1
Defeating Anxiety 1
Abstract 2
INTRODUCTION 6
PRINCIPLES 7
LESSON ONE 8
UNSAFE VS. SAFE SELF 8
LESSON 2 13
ANXIETY QUOTIENT QUIZ 13
    The Trap 18
    Unraveling the Trap 19
LESSON 3 21
EMOTIONAL ROLLER COASTER 21
    Stop this roller coaster and let me off. 21
LESSON 4 27
OBSESSIVE VS. TRUSTING 27
LESSON 5 31
HELPLESS TRAP AKA VICTIM MENTALITY 31
LESSON 6 37
PRISON CAMP OF ANXIETY 37
LESSON 7 41
ANXIETY VS. RESTING 41

LESSON 8	44
DISHRAG VS. STEEL	44
LESSON 9	49
DOUBLE MINDEDNESS VS. TRUSTWORTHY	49
CHAPTER 10	52
TRUE AND FALSE MATURITY	52
CHAPTER 11	57
ANXIETY HIDES SOMETHING	57
LESSON 12	61
PEACE	61
LEADER	64
SMALL GROUP RULES	65
LEADERSHIP GUIDELINES	66
GOOD FOLLOWER	68
AUTHOR'S BIOGRAPHIES	69
OTHER RESOURCES BY THE AUTHORS	70

INTRODUCTION

Foundationally our society is flawed and built on sinking sand. We must build our lives on solid ground with a **rock foundation** of emotional stability and strength to weather any storm. This is done through intentionally developing emotional maturity. Without this intentionality, intermittent emotional regression will dominate our lifespan. ***This teaching will give us the opportunity to train the next generation and turn them towards maturity and escape self-destructive behaviors. Exaggerated emotions leave us sick inside. This series will heal our souls.***

Developmental milestones in infancy are expected and even recorded in baby books. These physical milestones are rolling over, sitting up, crawling, walking, running, and talking. These innate abilities form naturally during growth. Physical milestones are easy to identify because they are visible. There are invisible emotional milestones that are as important as physical ones. Emotional milestones, if neglected, cannot only derail personal enjoyment and fulfillment of life's goals, but also sabotage every relationship and make life miserable. Emotional development can be stunted by trauma or instability in childhood.

Developmental emotional maturity is intentional mastering of our speech, thoughts, and actions. It is living above our emotions through the development of a sound mind. In this book, we will begin to explore the groundwork for achieving emotional milestones. These are not milestones that develop sequentially or naturally, but emotional maturity milestones that must be governed by intellect of the mind, courage of the heart, and intentionality. They do not come naturally but are developed by becoming ingrained into core emotional responses by conscious training.

PRINCIPLES

1) Be humble and lay down your burdens to find rest for your soul.
2) Emotions are a trap. KINDNESS is a gentle guide.
3) Give what you want to receive.
4) Worries and deceitfulness of riches choke the Word.
5) Take authority over your thoughts.
6) The truth sets you free.
7) Emotional resting is intentional; it is the opposite of anxiety.
8) Joy is a condition of the soul and is separate from our circumstances.
9) Focus on the destination and not the distractions.
10) Love makes lasting change.
11) Anxiety is a cover-up and hides root emotions.
12) Let peace guard your heart and mind in Christ Jesus.

LESSON ONE

UNSAFE VS. SAFE SELF

Introduction

- Our internal voice can be noisy.
- Learning to recognize your internal voice and take dominion over what it can say is a place of safety.
- Our world is not always safe or kind. However, we can always be kind to ourselves and others.
- This does not mean we are lazy, passive, or an excuse maker.
- It is quite the opposite; we will develop intentional awareness of our thinking patterns that drive our anxiety.
- If you have anxiety and no internal voice, you probably have stomach issues and other chronic aches and pains. If you are a non-thinker, you will need a safe place and safe people to help trace the breadcrumbs back to the lies you believe that cause the intense feelings of anxiety.

Lesson

Identify unsafe behaviors and intentionally develop safe behaviors.

Check the ones that apply to your inner self:	
Unsafe Inner Self An unsafe inner self:	
1) Starving for approval from others to validate yourself	
2) Gives in to peer pressure or conforms to expectations of others	
3) Self-abuse: alcohol, drugs, cutting, suicide thinking, etc.	
4) Self-destructive ("I do not care" attitude.)	
5) Abusive in relationships	
6) Sulky, broody, pouty, self-pity, whining	
7) Allows yourself to be abused	
8) Gives in to feelings of helplessness	
9) Feels worthless	
10) Attracts negative energy	

11) Stuck in a trauma cycle
12) Lives with unresolved grief
Results: isolation, rejection, self-neglect, abandonment of duty, and/or loneliness

Safe Inner Self A safe inner self:
1) Listens to feelings as a teacher but is not ruled by them
2) Does not speak negatively or put yourself or others down
3) Coaches yourself
4) Is gracious and kind to yourself
5) Gives grace to injuries and weakened parts of the body
6) Finds a place of peace

7) Is not easily provoked or out of balance	
8) Secure in who you are along your journey	
9) Can regulate emotional pain and rebalance quickly	
10) Follows a trusted path	
11) Develops good coping skills	
12) Develops community of trusted friends and acquaintances	
13) Practices humor	
14) Enjoys life	
Results: peace and self-acceptance	

Exercise

Choose one thing that is unsafe that burdens you that you want to stop doing and one thing that is safe that you want to work on today.

Application

Today, we will practice being safe for ourselves. This means you need to find things in the present to enjoy: a flower, a kitten, a child, a warm cup of tea, a soft pillow, a nice breeze, a sunny sky, etc.

Principle

Be humble and lay down your burdens to find rest for your soul (emotions). *Come to me, all you who are weary and burdened, and I will give you rest. Take my yoke upon you and learn from me, for I am gentle and humble in heart, and you will find rest for your souls. For my yoke is easy and my burden is light. Matthew 11:28-30*

Conclusion

As I separate my identity from my unsafe self and loved ones with dysfunctional behaviors, I can develop a new identity of a safe self. I can know who I am and determine how much I will and will not tolerate from myself or others. Sometimes, I take myself by the scruff of the neck and shake myself and say, "you will stop that!". If I am stuck in a toxic environment, I can empower myself by developing a plan of escape. I always have choices. I may not like them, but I have choices.

The Lord is my Rock, and my fortress and my deliverer, my God, my strength, in whom I trust... Psalm 18:2

O Lord, help me to lay down my burdens and find rest for my soul (emotions). Mature me to be safe for myself and safe for others to love me and enjoy my company. Help me to consciously choose to walk in humility and gentleness every day. In Jesus Name, Amen.

Write out your prayer:
Start with O God,
Help me...

LESSON 2

ANXIETY QUOTIENT QUIZ

Introduction

- Anxiety places us in the sympathetic nervous system. This is our flight or fight response.
- If this part of our brain is turned on constantly, no wonder we are suffering and exhausted emotionally.
- Today, we will examine our symptoms of anxiety and learn skills to stop those thoughts.
- When we learn to recognize anxiety, we can intentionally engage the calming parasympathetic nervous system.
- Freedom from anxiety is a reachable goal.

Lesson

There needs to be a decision to stop the anxiety, not to solve the problem.

These are easily identifiable symptoms of anxiety. You may find more. Mark ones that apply.

Emotional Symptoms	
• Anxious, nervous inside	
• Anger (explosive or seething)	
• Crying frequently	
• Hopeless/Helpless feelings	
• Despair	
• Fear	

Mental Symptoms	
• Short term memory loss	
• Lack of focus	
• Obsessing over problems-replaying drama	
• Revenge thoughts, plans or actions	
• Nightmares	

- Waking up tormented
- Confusion
- Fantasy thinking

Physical Symptoms
• Chronic Fatigue
• Stress induced illnesses
• Digestive Problems
• Choking on food, water, or swallowing difficulties
• Jaw clenching
• Frequent flus or colds
• Aches and pain
• Sleep problems

Relational Symptoms	
• Snippy, short with others	
• Impatient	
• Non-trusting	
• Isolation, withdraw	

Dysfunctional Behaviors	
• Self-destructive behaviors (cutting, substance use)	
• Compulsive speech (complaining, grumbling)	
• Overreacting (Aggressive)	
• Under-reacting (Avoidant or Doormat)	
• Paranoia	
• Impulsive	

• Binge eating, television, games
• Other dysfunctional self-comforting measures

Exercise

Name your greatest symptom of anxiety and give that problem to the Lord and speak a kind word to someone else. If you find you are anxious over the circumstance you released to the Lord, examine the situation for a few minutes. If you cannot fix it, release it to the Lord again.

Application

Anxiety is not you; it is just an emotion. Emotions are not to be followed. They have no intelligence. Matthew 15:14 *Leave them, they are blind guides. If a blind man leads a blind man, both will fall into a pit.* **Repeat after me:** "Emotions are Blind!" Do not follow emotions.

Principle

Emotions are a trap. KINDNESS is a gentle guide.

Anxiety weighs down the heart, but a kind word cheers it up.
Proverbs 12:25

THE TRAP

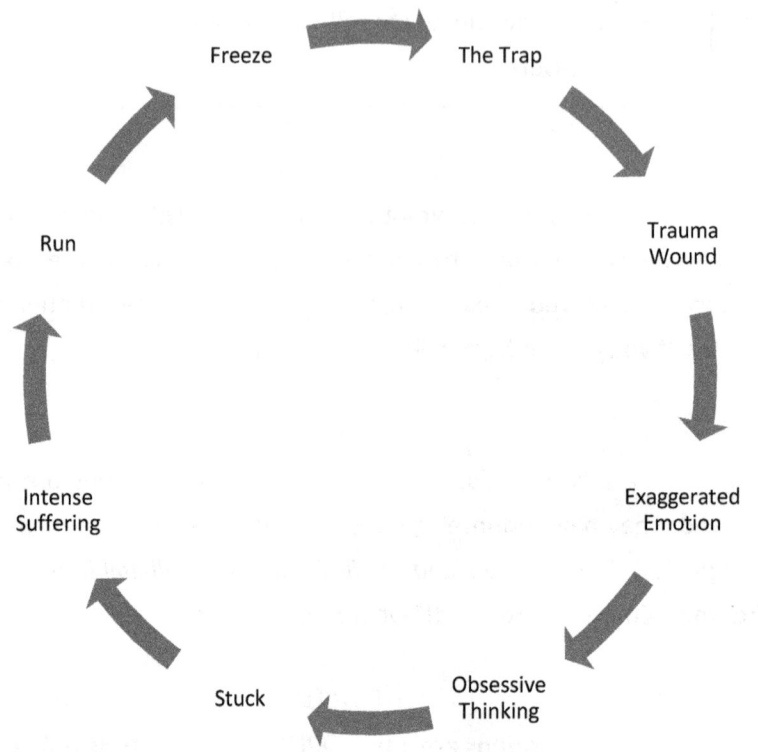

UNRAVELING THE TRAP

Conclusion

Recognize Triggers:

- what someone said or did,
- ·what thought you thought, or
- what lie you believed that caused you to be out of balance emotionally and feel unstable.

Wrestle your emotions to bring them under the control of your intelligent thinking to align with the **goals** you have established for yourself. For example: If a peer, boss, or other authority triggers an old wound and you sense an exaggerated emotion, instantly **BE KIND**. This will give you time and space to process what just happened and rebalance emotionally so you can grow and heal.

> **The Lord is my Rock, and my fortress and my deliverer, my God, my strength, in whom I trust… Psalm 18:2**

Lord, give me emotional intelligence to recognize my triggers, emotions, and corresponding thinking. Give me the self-control to be kind. Help me to think of others and how my words affect them. Give me grace. Give me freedom from anxiety. In Jesus Name. Amen.

Write out your prayer:
Start with O God,
Help me….

LESSON 3

EMOTIONAL ROLLER COASTER

CRISIS– TEMPORARY FIX – TEMPORARY RELIEF – CRISIS...

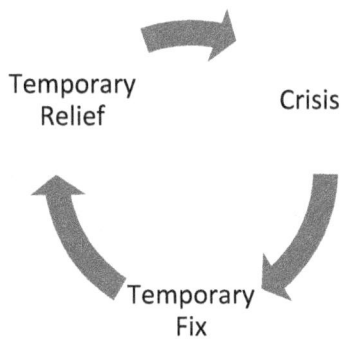

STOP THIS ROLLER COASTER AND LET ME OFF.

Introduction

- An emotional roller coaster is exhausting. There is never any real resolution.
- Any quick fix leads to another problem or a different crisis.
- Avoiding the hard work of maturing emotionally is usually only a temporary fix or temporary relief.
- Running away from the emotional pain of our temporary problem is impulsive and only stops the anxiety for a moment.
- Lasting resolutions come from stepping out of dysfunctional, exaggerated, and immature emotions and building lasting character changes through intentionally training your emotions and taking control of your life.

Lesson

Addictive Thinking Traps that make us powerless over anxiety. Learn to recognize them.

Addictive Thinking Traps	
1) Rationalizing	
2) Reasoning	
3) Obsessing over a person or situation	

4) Self-Pity	
5) Brooding and moody	
6) Angry or bitter	
7) Fearful or anxious	
8) Sulking and embracing melancholy	
9) No joy in the present moment	
10) Having to know future outcomes	
11) Needing to see the big picture and certain success before moving forward.	
12) Fairytale perfectionist daydreaming	

Exercise

Anxiety is a **STOP sign** to slow down and process life. What are your addictive thinking traps?

Application

Anxiety can be as simple as undisciplined thinking. Mental replay or obsessing over negativity or drama that you cannot control causes a rut in your brain and forms a habit. It leaches chemicals in your body that become addictive and you are incapable of stopping the constant replay. This could make anyone imbalanced or push them to dysfunctional behaviors to stop the suffering. We are going to learn a four-step process to correct our thinking.

Principle
Give what you want to receive.

Sowing and Reaping

Do not be deceived: God cannot be mocked. A man reaps what he sows. The one who sows to please his sinful nature, from that nature will reap destruction: the one who sows to please the Spirit, from the Spirit will reap eternal life. Galatians 6:7-8 Are you planting good or bad thoughts? What are you reaping?

What you give others, you receive.

Give, and it will be given to you. A good measure, pressed down, shaken together, and running over, will be poured into your lap. For with the measure you use, it will be measured to you. Luke 6:38 What is in your cup? You cannot pour goodness from a broken vessel.

Serve

Now that I, your Lord, and Teacher, have washed your feet, you also should wash one another's feet. I have set you an example that you should do as I have done for you. John 13:14-15 Who could you selflessly serve today without any expectation of return?

Develop Character

To this you were called, because Christ suffered for you, leaving you an example, that you should follow in his steps. 1 Peter 2:21

❖❖❖

Choose a character trait to work on today.

- Strong character needs to be chosen, practiced, and developed.
- Character will direct your thinking and stabilize your actions and reactions.
- Christ-like character of humility, truthfulness, loyalty, kindness, courage, obedience, respect, compassion, generosity, contentment, flexibility, orderliness, attentiveness, steadfastness, gratefulness, enthusiasm, endurance, determination, and dependability.

Conclusion

Mentally practice recognizing an addictive thought pattern. It is easier to stop <u>if you reject the thought within 3-5 seconds</u>. Recognize your thought patterns and practice working through the four steps. What am I sowing? What am I giving? Who am I serving? What character skill do I need to develop?

The Lord is my Rock, and my fortress and my deliverer, my God, my strength, in whom I trust... Psalm 18:2

Let me pray for you:

May the power of a living God flow into you. May God choose you to make known the glorious riches of this mystery, <u>which is Christ in you,</u> the hope of glory. (Colossians 1:27) May you be with Him who rides the ancient skies above and hear the thunders of His mighty voice (Psalms 68:33) and may you stop doubting and just believe. (John 20:27) In Jesus Name, Amen.

Write out your prayer:
Start with O God,
Help me...

LESSON 4

OBSESSIVE VS. TRUSTING

Introduction

- Prayer is work.
- Prayer is learned through dedication and practice.
- Prayer brings me close to the heart of God in fellowship.
- Prayer is a **total dependency and trust in God.**
- **Whatever you are thinking about controls you!**

Lesson

Today, I want you to learn to move from obsessive, anxious prayer to trusting, submissive and Scriptural prayer. Praying Scripture is the most powerful thing you can do to stop anxiety.

Obsessive Prayer

- Thoughts on the problem.
- Constantly replaying the problem in my mind.
- Rationalizing my actions in prayer.
- Wrestling with God and demanding He fix the problem.

Anxious Prayer

- Chronic worrying, fretful, crying, or fearful.

- Meditatively deciding how to manipulate circumstances to get my own way.
- Bargaining with God.
- Perverting Scripture to justify sinful behaviors.

Trusting & Submissive Prayer
- Allowing others to have free will to choose.
- Getting out of the way of violent, manipulative, angry people.
- Letting others have their own consequences or helping others with structure that requires them to be responsible, cooperative, and fully engaged in recovery.
- Honoring God first and setting strong, firm boundaries in relationships.
- Releasing loved ones and situations into God's faithful hands.

Scriptural Prayer
- Meditating on Scripture.
- Turning Scripture into prayers.
- Grateful for all things.
- Resting and waiting in Christ with full assurance of His sovereignty.
- Disciplined and scheduled prayer time.
- Intimacy and fellowship with Christ.
- Alert to pray for the needs of others.
- Purposefully praying for leaders and others in authority.

Exercise

What worry is consuming your life?

Application

Prayer is profound and yet somehow it is so simple that even a child can do it. Sometimes my prayers are so feeble, it is shocking how God answers exactly as I prayed for them. <u>Maybe it depends upon the depth of my obedience in hearing and receiving the Word</u> that my heavenly Father is concerned about more than any words that I might pray. *Others, like seed sown on good soil, hear the Word, accept it, and produce a crop—thirty, sixty or even a hundred times what was sown. Mark 4:20*

Principle

Worries and deceitfulness choke the Word.

"The worries of this life, and the deceitfulness of wealth, and the desires of other things (if allowed in my heart) come in and choke the Word, making it unfruitful." Mark 4:19

TURN THIS SCRIPTURE INTO PRAYER

Praying Scripture is the quickest and most powerful path to peace. God's Words are living and active and can discern our heart and cut through any confusion. *For the Word of God is living and active. Sharper than any double-edged sword, it penetrates even to dividing soul and spirit, joints, and marrow; it judges the thoughts and attitudes of the heart. Hebrews 4:12*

Lay your problems, sorrows, regrets on the altar of God. Ask Him to help you.

Scripture: *In you, O LORD, I have taken refuge; let me never be put to shame (confusion). Psalm 71:1*

Prayer: O Lord, stop the confusion. Please, give me refuge in You. Help me to make good decisions. Amen

Conclusion

- **Prayer does not work, if you do not pray.**
- **Pray earnestly.**
- **Pray fervently.**

The Lord is my Rock, and my fortress and my deliverer, my God, my strength, in whom I trust... Psalm 18:2

Dear God,

I am destitute, respond to my prayer. Do not despise my plea. Hear the groans of this prisoner and release me from condemnation. (Psalm 102:17,20) In Jesus Name, Amen.

Write out your prayer:
Start with O God,
Help me….

LESSON 5

HELPLESS TRAP AKA VICTIM MENTALITY

Introduction

- Sometimes, we can have the answer in our hands.
- We know what to do, but we do not understand how to apply the changes needed. For example, if we have a chronic illness, there is so much new information that can help us naturally heal our bodies. But if we think of ourselves as chronically ill, we may give up and stop searching for answers.
- This creates a helpless trap.
- Hope brings healing within our grasp.
- I want you to search for the answers to find your healing.
- The answers will become clear to us as we settle ourselves and slow down.
- Researching our problem for a hundred hours and trying a hundred things develops perseverance.

- If none of them work, more time may be needed, or a slower progress may be more realistic. We may have discovered a hundred things that do not work.
- The things that I tried years ago did not work. Now with more information, teaching, dedication, and perseverance, they are working.
- Just do not give up. Do not lose hope.

Lesson

Turn a helpless/victim mentality into a **life lesson of maturity.**

Victim mentality causes us suffering. Recognize this helpless thinking and refuse it. It only leads to more suffering. Circle the ones you recognize in your behaviors.

VICTIM THINKING	**DISCIPLINED THINKING**
Victim mentality (whining, complaining)	Disciplining my mind to change thinking patterns
Poor planning	Plan and prepare for change
Unpredictable circumstances	Flexible, expect the unexpected and make allowances for it
Blaming	Accepting responsibility for my actions
Excuse making	No excuses

All or nothing thinking	Balance
Fainthearted (giving up too quickly)	Steadfast and diligent
Fearful	Courageous
Anxious	Confident
Stressed	Relaxed
Constant worry	Trusting
Insomnia	Resting
Overeating	Disciplined eating
Under eating/anorexic	Healthy meals
Self-abuse (cutting, mind altering behaviors, gaming, binge television, irresponsible actions, lacking self-care, etc.)	Self-care (exercise, healthy diet, healthy thinking, counseling if needed, community of caring friends)
I will never be better	I can do this!

Nothing will ever help me	I can be patient while I search for answers
I will never overcome this injury, illness, addiction, or diagnosis	I can improve in many areas, and keep working and be hopeful with stubborn issues
I am hopeless	I am full of hope
I feel like giving up	No retreat
Frequently have feelings of depression	Empowered through disciplining my thinking and separating my identity from my irrational thinking
Suicidal thinking	Suicidal thinking is not an option. I refuse to go there.

Exercise

Name a victim behavior and exchange it for a discipline in your thinking and incorporate it today.

Application

It is a simple shift. Not easy, but simple. It is taking dominion over your thinking and forcing victim thinking out of your mind.

Principle

You can take authority over your thoughts.

The weapons we fight with are not the weapons of the world. On the contrary, they have divine power to demolish strongholds. We demolish arguments and every pretension that sets itself up against the knowledge of God, and we <u>take captive every thought</u> to make it obedient to Christ. 2 Corinthians 10:4-5

Conclusion

As much as we would like to do it, we cannot break through the mental blockage of someone else's *helpless trap*. We can help them develop a plan, but they must set up accountability. They may have to be sick of suffering to be motivated for lasting change.

If we give our loved ones the tools to change their thinking, we can wait for them to be sick of suffering and ready to do the work change requires. Sometimes, it takes a decade before they move towards change.

We can stop our whine. We can lead the way. If we show them health and emotional stability is within our grasp, our loved ones may follow and pursue health and well-being.

The Lord is my Rock, and my fortress and my deliverer, my God, my strength, in whom I trust… Psalm 18:2

Dear God, save me from being a helpless victim. May I be free from the enemy's trap. May the trap be permanently broken. May I permanently, totally and completely escape and develop disciplined thinking. In Jesus Name, Amen.

Write out your prayer:
Start with O God,
Help me....

LESSON 6

PRISON CAMP OF ANXIETY

Introduction

> *Anxiety is a prison camp of suffering; it is within your power to stop it!*

Anxiety captures you in the bondage of suffering:
- Until you recognize your behavioral dysfunctions that cover your deep inner wounds.
- Until you stop trying to change people and situations you cannot change.
- Until you stop identifying with broken circumstances.

Lesson

Stop being your own enemy and build the identity as a warrior!

In what ways are you your own enemy?

If you are entertaining anxiety, you are on the enemy's side of the battle. You are tearing down and destroying your own life with anxiety. This behavior steals the enjoyment of today. It robs you of your health. Anxiety keeps you distracted from things which matter. Anxiety's weapons are fear, worry, discouragement and confusion.

- **What you believe about a situation is powerful.**
- **What you say to yourself about a circumstance is powerful.**
- **Do not elevate your emotions to the level of truth.**

Build your identity in Christ and fight anxiety with truth!

Truth

- I am fearfully and wonderfully made. Psalm 139:14
- I am made in the image of a mighty God. Genesis 1:26
- I can do all things through Christ who strengthens me. Romans 8:28
- I am more than a conqueror through Christ who loves me. Romans 8:37
- There is nothing that can separate me from the love of God, not death, nor life, nor angels, nor demons, nor powers, nor things present, nor things to come. Romans 8:35
- **Absolutely nothing** can separate me from my God's love: not trouble, not hardship or persecution, famine, nakedness, danger, or a sword like anxiety that was intended to destroy me. Romans 8:38
- **Nothing can come between you and Christ!**
- **Anxiety takes you captive in a prison camp. The bars of your cage are the lies you believe.**
- **Get up and fight for your freedom. You are worth it!**

Exercise

What lie do you need to renounce? What truth do you need to believe?

Application

Memorize one of the truths of your identity and say it 100 times a day.

Anxiety is just undisciplined emotions. It is a warning light on the dashboard of life to show you something in your thinking that needs examined, worked through, corrected, and released.

Principle

The truth sets you free.

...you will know the truth, and the truth will set you free. John 8:32

Conclusion

It is your **passive thinking** that must be reeled in. If you are not purposeful about what you are thinking, anxiety will capture you and every moment will be filled with stress. It takes a purposeful training of your mind to build a new identity and reject all anxious thoughts. This is war against passive thinking on enemy ground! Fight for your freedom from anxiety!

Do not rob yourself of the chance to mature, grow and experience victory in overcoming self-imposed burdens of poor decision making. These anxieties turned into responsibilities and firmly placed on your shoulders might be the very weight you need to correct yourself.

The Lord is my Rock, and my fortress and my deliverer, my God, my strength, in whom I trust... Psalm 18:2

Dear God,

Sovereign Lord, you have begun to show your servant your greatness and your strong hand. For what god is there in heaven or on earth who can do the deeds and mighty works you do? I do believe; help me overcome my unbelief. (Deuteronomy 3:24; Mark 9:24) In Jesus Name, Amen.

Write out your prayer:
Start with O God,
Help me....

LESSON 7

ANXIETY VS. RESTING

Introduction

- Rest is a peace of mind and spirit.
- This is an emotional rest, not necessarily a physical one.
- Free from anxiety and disturbance
- Confident and trusting

Isaiah 30:15 In <u>repentance</u> and <u>rest</u> you will find your salvation; in <u>quietness</u> and <u>confidence</u> you will find your strength.

Lesson

1) Repenting means doing a complete turn from unbelief.

Hebrews 3:12-13 *See to it, brothers, that none of you has a <u>sinful, unbelieving heart</u> that turns away from the living God. But encourage one another daily, as long as it is called Today, so that none of you may be hardened by sin's deceitfulness.*

2) Resting means stopping your own work.

Hebrews 4:10 *For anyone who enters God's rest also rests from his own work, just as God did from His.*

3) The inability to "rest" emotionally from anxiety means I have unbelief.

Hebrews 4:6 It still remains that some will enter that rest, and those who formerly had the gospel preached to them did not go in, because of their disobedience (unbelief).

4) Quietness means being still inside.

Psalm 46:10 Be still and know that I am God.

5) Confidence means trusting completely and totally in God, no matter what!

Proverbs 3:26 For the Lord will be your confidence and will keep your foot from being snared.

Exercise

Let anxiety remind you to find a quiet place to trust. What would it look like to exchange anxiety for trust? Trusting God allows us to be emotionally quiet where we can rest. My favorite words to release me from anxiety and move me into trusting God is "Well Lord, I just can't wait to see what you are going to do with this one!

Application

God rested on the seventh day. Not because he was tired, but for an example to us. Physical resting is the opposite of working or striving. **Emotional resting is the opposite of anxiety.**

Hebrews 4:3-4,6-7 (3) ...now we who have believed enter into that rest (but) just as God has said, "So I declared on oath in my anger, 'They shall never enter my rest.'" (4) And yet his work has been finished since the creation of the world. And on the seventh day God rested from all his work.: (6) they did not go in because of their disobedience (unbelief). **Instructions** *(7) "Today, if you hear his voice, do not harden your hearts."*

> *Could a hardened heart be an anxious heart?*

Principle

Emotional resting is intentional. It is the opposite of anxiety.

Hebrews 4:10 For anyone who enters God's rest also rests from their works, just as God did from his.

Conclusion

<u>Resting is a maturity skill.</u> Maturity depends on the stronger part of ourselves. We can create a dialogue within our hearts to find a place of safety. When I become **aware** of my anxiety, I am to **acknowledge** it and then act. The action to take is "believing". Release yourself from the responsibility to fear, fret or worry. Just be concerned enough to do the next right thing and have faith that other things will work themselves out.

The Lord is my Rock, and my fortress and my deliverer, my God, my strength, in whom I trust... Psalm 18:2

Dear God,

Forgive me for my arrogance and pride that has hardened my heart. Let me be your clay and You, O God, my potter. Form and shape me into Your image. In Jesus Name, Amen.

Write out your prayer:
Start with O God,
Help me….

LESSON 8

DISHRAG VS. STEEL

Introduction

There is a mentality that repeats itself over and over without resolution. This feels like a wet dishrag. We are soaking up all the spills around us, good or bad. It is time to learn to discern what you will allow in your mind and not to allow anything to control you other than the truth of God's Word and right thinking. This is what I call becoming "steel".

Jeremiah is complaining to the Lord and even calls God a liar. The Lord corrects the prophet Jeremiah and instructs him to not align himself with the wicked (unbelievers), but to re-align himself with God. Then God will be able to make the prophet like a fortified brazen wall.

Jeremiah 15: 18-20 (Jeremiah is speaking to God.) (18) Why is my pain perpetual, and my wound incurable, which refuses to be healed? Will you be altogether unto me as a liar, and as waters that fail? (19) Therefore this says the Lord, If you return, then will I bring you again, and you shall stand before me: and if you take forth the precious (worthy) from the vile (unworthy), you will be as my mouth... (20) And I will make you unto this people a <u>fenced brazen wall</u>:...for I am with you and will deliver (rescue) you, says the Lord. (KJV)

Lesson

Identify and correct your attitudes of unbelief. Separate what is precious (worthy) in your life from what is vile (unworthy).

Where is your focus?

Detach from a temporary earthly focus and attach to an eternal godly focus. This is intentional. It does not come easy; we must wrestle our thoughts and choose which ones are beneficial for us to think and which ones are not and reject the thoughts that cause our suffering. If we focus on the temporary, we will have travail and vexation; if we focus on what is really important for eternity, we will have a quiet heart. (Ecclesiastes 4:6)

The psalmist starts many psalms with his feelings, and he unloads his troubles. Frequently, he complains and asks, "God, where are you?" Then he remembers who he is talking to and he settles down. He changes from this wet, dishrag mentality of wrestling with his own internal anguish into faithfulness and hope. This is how he does it.

"I keep my eyes always on the Lord. With him at my right hand, I will not be shaken" (Psalm 16:8)

He shifts his focus from the temporal things he cannot control, and he focuses on the eternal goodness of God.

Exercise

As you read through the psalms, <u>note</u> the behaviors, or negative circumstances of the people around the psalmist. <u>Identify</u> feelings the psalmist experiences and the thoughts he allows himself to think. He speaks to himself until he changes his feelings into the solid foundation of truth of the attributes of God.

Psalm 16:
The Psalmist David's thoughts:

God keeps me safe.

God is my refuge.

You are my Lord, apart from you I have no good thing.

Lord is my portion.

Lord is my cup.

Lord makes me secure.

Lord places me in pleasant places.

Lord counsels me.

Lord instructs me.

David's commitment following his thoughts:

I will delight in holy people.

I will look for a delightful inheritance.

I will praise the Lord.

I will keep my eyes on the Lord.

Results:

My heart is glad.

My tongue rejoices.

My body rests secure.

I am filled with joy in God's presence.

I have God's eternal pleasures.

Truth (David's observations):

Running after other gods causes suffering.

David's commitment:

I will not sacrifice to other gods.

I will not even mention their names.

Where is David's God?

God is at my right hand.

David was privileged to see the messianic future of Christ. I believe this is for all of us who follow God.

God will not abandon me.

God keeps His faithful ones.
God makes me know the path of life.

Application

Situations are the same but now the psalmist David has taken dominion or authority over the ground that is within his soul.

No longer will he tolerate being tossed around by circumstances. Instead, he fills it with the love of God. Now he can find contentment, peace, quietness, and stillness within his soul. The psalmist settles on the attributes of a merciful and loving God and he only seeks to know and trust in his God to save him. As he does this, **his circumstances may or may not change, but he changes.**

Principle

Joy is a condition of the soul and is separate from our circumstances.

Conclusion

Happiness is temporary, allusive, and based on circumstances. True and lasting joy is as deep as eternity. David found the secret to maintaining this lasting joy. It is in thinking high thoughts about God and trusting totally in Him.

Psalm 15 David conveys how to never be shaken. Psalm 17 he pleads with God about his circumstances and he ends the chapter with wanting to be conformed into the image of God. Psalm 17:15 has become my life verse.

As for me, I will behold thy face in righteousness: I shall be satisfied, when I awake, with thy likeness. Psalm 17:15 KJV

> *Ask God for a "life verse". One that is powerful enough to give you strength in the darkest night.*

The Lord is my Rock and my fortress, and my deliverer; my God, my strength, in whom I trust... Psalm 18:2

My Lord and my God hear me,

Let me never be shaken no matter what my circumstances. Let me see your face in righteousness and let me never be satisfied until I awake in your likeness. (Psalm 17:15 KJV) In Jesus Name, Amen.

Write out your prayer:
Start with O God,
Help me....

LESSON 9

DOUBLE MINDEDNESS VS. TRUSTWORTHY

Introduction

Doublemindedness makes us unstable and tossed to and fro. It causes confusion and instability. Then we can be easily blown off course and end up on a turbulent sea of raging waters and be pushed towards an ocean of consequences. Doubt makes us double minded and unstable. Instead, be intentional, like a sea captain, and chart your course.

James 1:6-8 (6) But when he asks, he must believe and not doubt, because he who doubts is like a wave of the sea, blown and tossed by the wind. (7) That man should not think he will receive anything from the Lord; (8) he is a double-minded man, unstable in all he does.

Lesson

1) **The greatest skill you will learn is to say "no" to yourself.** Build your stamina. Practice consistently being honest in the little things.

Luke 16:10 "Whoever can be trusted with very little can also be trusted with much, and whoever is dishonest with very little will also be dishonest with much."

2) **Do not trust your own thinking.**

Proverbs 12:15 The way of a fool seems right to him, but a wise man listens to advise.

3) **Unravel confusion by asking the Lord for your teachers.**

Isaiah 30:20-21 (20) Although the Lord gives you the bread of adversity and the water of affliction, your teachers will be hidden no more, with your own eyes you will see them. (21) Whether you turn to the right or to the left, your ears will hear a voice behind you saying, "This is the way; walk in it."

4) **Ask Yourself:**
- Is this a responsible decision?
- Will this help me attain my goals for maturity?
- Will this harm anyone else?
- Am I being impulsive or selfish?
- Have I asked for counsel from mature, trusted leaders?

Exercise

Identify your good counselors. Identify your trusted teachers.

Application

Doublemindedness is painful and sometimes causes us to make irrational, impulsive decisions. This may include running from painful recovery work. It may require us to be accountable for foolish decisions and accepting hard consequences.

If you do not know what decision to make, DO NOT DO ANYTHING UNTIL IT BECOMES CLEAR! What circumstances are causing you to be distracted and anxious? What would it look like to become responsible in all the small areas of your life?

Principle

Focus on the destination and not the distractions.

Conclusion

Do not doubt that you can recover. Do the work. Place boundaries on your behaviors. Submit to authority. Return and apologize often. Build a trustworthy character that you and others can depend on.

The Lord is my Rock and my fortress, and my deliverer; my God, my strength, in whom I trust... Psalm 18:2

O God,

Let me be responsible, dependable, and accountable to do what I ought to do when I ought to do it. Let me be found faithful. (1 Corinthians 4:2) In Jesus Name, Amen.

Write out your prayer:
Start with O God,
Help me....

CHAPTER 10

TRUE AND FALSE MATURITY

Introduction

Unless we can identify the difference between true and false maturity, it is impossible to know if we are beginning to develop emotional soundness. As we begin to understand the hard work of emotional maturity, we can identify the lies we believe and confront them. We will most likely need to use all the strength we have to stop our denial and understand the battle we are fighting.

Lesson

Circle your behaviors. Do they represent true or false maturity?

True Maturity	**False Maturity**
Broken heart... grieving over any emotional outburst	Sorry for consequences, not behavior

Apologizing to anyone you have wronged	Lots of emotions, crying, anger, mood swings
Setting boundaries to prevent themselves from falling back into old habits	Good behavior (temporarily) to make up for wrongs
Setting up accountability partners	Self-destructive thinking/behaviors
Being open and accountable in every area of life	Saying "I am sorry." No plan to change
Confessing past wrongs (with trusted person), planning for restitution	Makes excuses (hiding full truth/blaming others)
Seeking help	Weasels out of consequences
Sticking to a plan developed by counselor/authority	Refusing to talk over issues, "No one tells me what to do." Demands blind trust
Walking daily in emotional maturity	Playing a good game, while they are learning to manipulate outcomes

Serving others without a desire for reward or a motive to manipulate others	Justifying self and grandiose thinking, they only do chores or favors with a motive to manipulate for selfish gain
Placing structure in life. Make bed, take out trash, fold laundry, do the dishes, etc.	Avoids responsibility
Schedule (work)	Embezzles money and cons elderly or weak for money, Misuses money allotted
Earns relationship trust one day at a time	Escalates emotions to cast confusion
Looks for a reason for past failures and working through past wounds to find healing	Creates crisis and diversion, (Self-destructive behaviors), runs away, cuts self, threatens suicide
Finds healthy social settings	Returns to dysfunctional friends
Works towards developing boundaries to establish a safe environment	Resents submitting to authority

Corrects self by confessing and asks for forgiveness often	Double talks
Speaks truth even if there are consequences	Lies
Accepts responsibility for actions	Blames
Provides for self and pays what has been borrowed, cares for their children or elderly parents	Selfish, bullies, dominates, plays a victim

Exercise

Think of the last thing you said, "I am sorry" about and ask yourself, "Have I made provision in my life for a change?"

Application

- **Emotional maturity without behavioral change is not maturity.**
- True maturity is a turning away from destructive behaviors and then turning towards something valuable.
- **Remember:** Love makes lasting changes...
- Selfish people follow the direction of pleasing only themselves....

Principle

Love makes lasting change.

"...love covers over all wrongs." Proverbs 10:12

Conclusion

Some relationships are toxic and need strong boundaries and distance.

Sometimes we cannot apologize:
- If I repent to a bully for upsetting them, I can expect they will test me with another outrageous demand.
- I must say no and set up boundaries, otherwise, they will heat up the rage to prove that I am the unrepentant one.

Truth: Repentance should never give someone else the upper hand to manipulate me... again.

The Lord is my Rock and my fortress, and my deliverer; my God, my strength, in whom I trust... Psalm 18:2

O God,

You, O Lord, can keep my lamp burning; my God turns my darkness into light. Let me crush the enemy's army and have the strength to scale a wall to escape. Let me walk blameless before you and keep myself from sin. (Psalm 18:23,28,29) In Jesus Name, Amen.

Write out your prayer:
Start with O God,
Help me....

CHAPTER 11

ANXIETY HIDES SOMETHING

Introduction

Learn that anxiety is only a curtain to hide another emotion that is overwhelming. I woke up this morning brewing with anxiety. So, I sat with the Lord and asked Him why I was so anxious. Then I went through my feelings word list and when I landed on sadness the tears flowed.

Sadness and grieving were uncovered; now, I can be **aware** of the sadness, **acknowledge** it and choose to **act** on processing sadness and start working through it. <u>This immediately resolved my anxiety.</u>

My dear friend died a few days ago and I miss him terribly and have not processed the loss. This emotion of sadness for him could be overwhelming, but instead, I will sit with it and allow myself to feel it a little every morning, until peace replaces the sadness.

Learn to recognize the feeling of anxiety. Whenever I am stuck in anxiety or any other strong emotion for more than two weeks, it is time to admit it and reach out for help. Obviously, I am not going to figure this out on my own and it will soon become toxic and be driven to dysfunction if not resolved.

Lesson

1) Unresolved anxiety drives us to dysfunctional behavior to try to rebalance ourselves.

2) Resolving anxiety with poor coping skills is only a temporary fix and results in compounded problems.

3) Avoiding responsibilities is not a way to avoid anxiety.

4) Underlying chronic anxiety makes us prone to overreact in defensiveness or panic and flee during any minor confrontation which causes us to lose our employment, maturity progress, and other structures of stability (warm, loving relationships and healthy friendships).

5) Dysfunctional behaviors or even suicidal thinking is just an attempt to rebalance the inner soul from dysregulated emotions.

Feelings Word Lists: *nervous, fearful, worried, fretful, hopeless, helpless, bullied, irritated, frustrated, confused, angry, stubbornness, bitterness, hatred, abandoned, betrayed, neglected, misunderstood, rejected, insecure, unloved, unwanted, judged, condemned, embarrassed, trapped, lonely, self-pity, hurt, sad, grieving, overwhelmed, depressed or suicidal.*

Exercise

When you feel anxious, sit with it quietly for a moment and go through this feeling word list and uncover the emotion that has not been processed and resolved.

Application

Some emotions are so strong when you allow yourself to feel them that they cause intense suffering. I want you to feel these emotions a little at a time and process them with a trusted friend or sponsor. Journaling can help move emotions from inside of you to outside where they will not be so intense. If you are numb and cannot feel anything, you have learned to stop all emotions to function in daily life. When these emotions get turned back on, they may be very scary. Be in charge and set a timer and feel the intense emotions for 5-10 minutes and then get up and enjoy your day. If they overwhelm you again, do this:

1) Get alone.
2) Set the timer 5-10 minutes.
3) Feel the emotion intensely.
4) Push it outside of you and do not identify with it.
5) Get up and enjoy your day.

Emotions are just emotions; they are not YOU! DO NOT IDENTIFY WITH YOUR EMOTIONS OR THEY WILL RULE YOU! Be aware of emotions. Then acknowledge emotions and act by feeling them and processing them a little at a time.

Principle

Anxiety is a cover-up and hides root emotions.
"...for I am full of shame (confusion); and drowned in my afflictions."
(Job 10:15b)

Conclusion

Unprocessed emotions come out some other way. Some of this work only you can do. No one can handle all your unresolved accumulated pain. Choose 3-4 dependable people and build strong relationships with them so you feel like you have many people to share your burdens. Some emotions are built into problems. The problem does not need to be solved for the emotion to be resolved.

So, you say, "If I start feeling this emotion, my suffering will never stop." I am here to tell you that it will. You can oversee your emotions by finding a quiet place every day and processing them a few minutes at a time. One day you will wake up and find the emotion of peace.

The Lord is my Rock and my fortress, and my deliverer; my God, my strength, in whom I trust... Psalm 18:2

O God,

Fill me with knowledge of your will through all spiritual wisdom and understanding. Let me live a life worthy of you. Let me please you in every way. Let me be strengthened with all power according to your glorious might so that I might have great endurance and patience and joyfully give thanks to the Father. (Colossians 1:9,10) In Jesus Name, Amen.

Write out your prayer:
Start with O God,
Help me....

LESSON 12

PEACE

Introduction

Peace hides behind problems. Problems are common to this world.
Where is my peace?
>Where is my peace?
>How can it so easily elude me?
>I know it is a gift, so does it come in a box?
>How does it get away so quickly?
>Does it have legs to run on?
>Does it hide behind my problem or under the bed?
>How can it be so near, yet be oh so very far?
>How can it be so hard to find, but oh so easy to lose?

Turn from evil and do good; seek peace and pursue it. Psalm 34:14

Lesson

- There is a cure for anxiety.
- It is not easy, but simple.
- It is a moment by moment choice to do the next right thing.

- Now refuse anxiety and replace it with gratefulness.

Do not be anxious about anything, but in everything, by <u>prayer and petition,</u> with <u>thanksgiving</u>, present your <u>requests</u> to God.

Exercise

Let peace reign in your heart by turning every anxious thought into a grateful one. This does not mean you are grateful for bad things, but for the opportunities to see everything meant for evil to be turned into good.

Genesis 50:20 You intended to harm me, but God intended it for good to accomplish what is now being done and saving of many lives.

Application

Do not be anxious about anything, instead, be grateful.

This is a journey. We are growing and learning. Gratefulness changes our focus. In my nursing career, I have stood by the bed of dying saints who are in total peace glorifying God. So, the presence of anxiety does not depend upon circumstance or on the fallen state of this world.

Anxiety is my lack of understanding of who I am in Christ and the work of salvation he is doing in me and how to use His blessed resources available to me.

Principle

Let peace guard your heart and mind in Christ Jesus.

And the peace of God, which transcends all understanding, will guard your hearts and your minds in Christ Jesus. Philippians 4:6-7

Conclusion

- Perhaps I have never been taught how to trust Christ in every area of my life.
- Perhaps I never knew true peace abides only in a trusting relationship with my Lord.
- Perhaps I have not understood how to go into my prayer closet and shut the door to anxiety and the outside world.

Discover the mystery of the hidden chamber.

Psalms 51:6 Surely you desire truth in the inner parts; you teach me wisdom in the inmost place (hidden chamber).

The Lord is my Rock and my fortress, and my deliverer; my God, my strength, in whom I trust. Psalm 18:2

O God,

Rescue me from the dominion of darkness. Give me a share of the inheritance of the saints in the kingdom of light. Thy kingdom come; thy will be done. (Colossians 1:12,13; Matthew 6:10) In Jesus Name, Amen.

Write out your prayer:
Start with O God,
Help me....

LEADER

1) Print pdf from angiegmeadows.com website.

2) Open in prayer.

3) Review Group Rules.

4) Review last lesson. Ask how they were able to apply it to their life and any success or failures they experienced.

5) Teach your own presentation using the material. Or preview the Rock of Recovery podcast/Angie G Meadows YouTube to see if this discussion is appropriate for your group. Watch for new podcast/YouTube general anxiety recovery.

6) Go through the lesson one point at a time for open discussion.

7) If group is over 8-12 members, split it up into smaller groups for discussion, if you want to do so. Train your stronger believers for co-leader support positions.

8) Give examples of how God helped you solve the problem.

9) End the group in prayer (Take prayer requests or have a basket for them to write out a written request and ask them to mark the request "private" or "public").

10) If time allows, add an opportunity for those with heavy burdens to stay longer for encouragement and prayer.

SMALL GROUP RULES

1) Give everyone an opportunity to speak.

2) Keep the discussion to the topic.

3) We are not here to "fix" each other. We are here to support and encourage one another.

4) If you do not want to share, simply say "pass" when it comes to your turn.

5) It is vital that this is a safe place for everyone. No negative, judgmental, or condemning comments. The Rule is LOVE!

6) Confidentiality is mandatory and is taken very seriously.

7) Whatever is spoken in this room, stays in this room.

8) If during the week, you discuss another member's comments among one another, it is to be in the spirit of prayer and encouragement and not in mockery or ridicule. No gossiping or slandering will be tolerated.

9) There will be a release of anyone who wants to leave after the lesson and discussion time.

10) There will often be added extra time of sharing at the end of the group for those with heavy burdens who want to share their struggles and receive individual prayer or for those who want to stay and encourage those struggling.

LEADERSHIP GUIDELINES

Dishonorable Leadership	Honorable Leadership
Anger	Happy Countenance
Use of fear tactics	Approachable
Threats/Bullying	Patient and Kind
Retaliation for being confronted	Gracious; holds others accountable
Hasty/Rash	Treats everyone the same
Impatient	Good self-identity
Arrogant	Good boundaries
Values self, money, or project goals more than others	Good mentors Good relationships
Holds a grudge	Unemotional decision maker
Plays favorites	Leads through serving

Casts confusion on situations to blame shift	Humble-Leads with power and under submission to their authority
Makes emotional decisions not principally based decisions	Will do what is right, no matter the consequences
Denies problems	Good listener
Deals only with superficial problems	Forgives easily; coaches weaker ones; encourages others.
Ignores the main problem	Identifies root problems
Does not seek counsel	Seek many counselors
Ask impossible things	Able to plan and develop goals
Unrealistic/Demanding	Able to follow through with a plan
*Adapted from observation of the behaviors of Nebuchadnezzar the pagan king in the book of Daniel.	Always same level of emotional availability

No bullying or verbal abuse ever!
Kind, but firm!

GOOD FOLLOWER

1. Respects Authority
2. Protects Good Name
3. Learns to Stand Alone (not follow a crowd)
4. Guards the truth
5. Takes responsibility for actions
6. Honorable and fair in decisions
7. Makes good sound financial decisions
8. Lives with Self-Control
9. Moderation in all things
10. Gives good days work without complaint
11. Always on time; dependable
12. Never gossips, slanders, or accuses
13. Takes any issues up the ladder through the chain of command
14. Guards all that is entrusted into their hands; trustworthy
15. Refuses to do anything illegal, unethical, or immoral

*You must learn to be a good follower to be a good leader.

AUTHOR'S BIOGRAPHIES

Angie G Meadows graduated from St Mary's School of Nursing as a Registered Nurse, Marshall University with a Bachelor's in Nursing and Ohio State University with a Master's in Nursing. She has worked at multiple hospitals in multiple capacities. Angie has been a keen observer of human behaviors as she has dealt with enablers and loved ones with Substance Use Disorder over the years. She is currently a wife, mother, speaker, and writer. Her favorite pastime is quilting.

Sarah J Meadows graduated from Liberty University with a bachelor's degree in psychology. She has worked in the public-school system as a Therapeutic Day Treatment Counselor. She is currently pursuing a master's degree in clinical Mental Health Counseling. Sarah enjoys her friends and her beloved corgi.

OTHER RESOURCES BY THE AUTHORS

A Thousand Tears: An Enabler's Journey ISBN 9781732810204

https://www.amazon.com/Thousand-Tears-Enablers-Journey/dp/1732810206

This is the same book as Enabler's Journey: A Christian Perspective, but it is written with principles and not Scriptures.

The book identifies the Enabler's Cycle and our conflict with individuals with addiction. Identifying manipulative, devouring, or toxic relationships in our life and learning to confront and detach. This book is a useful tool in dealing with persons with substance use disorder or abusive loved ones. It also includes multiple self-assessment tools: Enabler's paradigm, entanglement gauge, anxiety quotient, trust scales, and much more.

An Enabler's Journey: A Christian Perspective ISBN: 9781732810211

https://read.amazon.com/kp/embed?asin=B07KDK1L1F&preview=newtab&linkCode=kpe&ref_=cm_sw_r_kb_dp_aaEgFbPSB9P11 Book preview.

https://www.amazon.com/Enablers-Journey-Christian-Perspective-ebook/dp/B07KDK1L1F/ref=pd_sim_351_2/147-3762080-9342150?_encoding=UTF8&pd_rd_i=B07KDK1L1F&pd_rd_r=58dcb7aa-921e-4665-b6f0-ce42ced569ff&pd_rd_w=fau3o&pd_rd_wg=wWRbM&pf_rd_p=6f740e39-0c25-4380-8008-7a4156dab959&pf_rd_r=3W4KGCECXB8C6AVDAQJ0&psc=1&refRID=3W4KGCECXB8C6AVDAQJ0

This book is 300+ pages and 24 chapters. It is almost the same book as *A Thousand Tear: An Enabler's Journey* except it has a 100+ Scriptures to validate the principles for dealing with people in relationships.

Enabler's Journey Recovery Plan: Enabler's Journey Recovery Series: Book 1 ISBN: 9781732810228

https://www.amazon.com/Enablers-Journey-Recovery-Plan-Book-ebook/dp/B07NTND743/ref=sr_1_1?dchild=1&keywords=angie+g+meadows&qid=1590167957&s=books&sr=1-

This is a 100+ page Book One of a recovery workbook series. It guides individuals and clients to understand enabling behaviors and evaluate their current participation in perpetuating a person with substance use disorder's illness. The enabler will learn to recognize the cycle of enabling, entanglement, excuses, and beliefs that handicap an enabler from recovery. It also coaches in the courage needed for detaching from destructive people and circumstances we cannot control. The book includes an enabler's recovery plan, accountability questionnaire, self-care program and a plan for identifying unhealthy and healthy coping strategies. It will also guide the recovering enabler to determine a level of safe involvement with a person with substance use disorder and how to identify true and false recovery, rebuild trust, and avoid the snare of another enabling relationship. It will help us recognize dysfunctional thinking and our false belief system that keeps us entangled. There are 5 chapters from the original *A Thousand Tears: An Enabler's Journey* book and 3 extra in-depth recovery chapters and many added self-evaluation charts. This is a beginner book or small group book for an Enabler. It is short and concise with lots of diagrams and easy to understand flowcharts. It is a great beginner tool with lots of reflective questions for counsellors or small groups to use in guiding enablers to recovery.

Enabler's Journey Detachment: Enabler's Journey Recovery Series Book 2 ISBN: 9781732810235

https://www.amazon.com/Enablers-Journey-Detachment-Recovery-Book-ebook/dp/B07RQWP5YR/ref=sr_1_fkmr0_2?dchild=1&keywords=angie+g+meadows+detachment&qid=1590168176&s=digital-text&sr=1-2-fkmr0

This book empowers us to learn survival skills with 12 DETACHMENT PRINCIPLES. The spiraling financial consequences, mental anguish, emotional chaos, and physical drain of enabling begs the voice of detachment to ensure self-preservation. This book is a useful tool in dealing with Substance Use Disorder, or other individuals with abusive or irresponsible behaviors. It includes many self-assessment tools: Entitlement Evaluation, Empowerment Plan, Helpless Trap, Healthier Me, Healthy Speech Evaluation, Negative Emotional Triggers, Unmet Needs, Obsessive Thinking Traps, Forgiveness, Bitterness, Reconciliation, Holidays, Suffering, Power to Stop Enabling, Self-Talk, Rules for Survival, practical steps, reflective

www.ingramcontent.com/pod-product-compliance
Lightning Source LLC
Chambersburg PA
CBHW031420040426
42444CB00005B/654